GOOD
SAINT
JOHN
XXIII

Published by Clear Faith Publishing LLC
22 Lafayette Rd
Princeton, NJ 08540

ISBN 978-1-9404-1408-9

First Printing April, 2014

Cover & Interior Design by Doug Cordes

Illustrations by Brother Mickey O'Neill McGrath

Good Saint John XXIII is printed on 100# Influence Matte #3 and the text is set in Source Sans Pro and Lynx.

Printed in the Canada

Judy

GOOD

SAINT

JOHN

XXIII

Be a joyful saint!

Mickey McGrath
2018

FOREWORD

JAMES MARTIN, SJ

Michael O'Neill McGrath, OSFS, universally known as "Mickey" or "Brother Mickey," is one of the finest and most beloved Christian artists of our age. His new book on Saint John XXIII is a beautiful addition to what is becoming an important artistic legacy.

Mickey and I came to know one another perhaps 20 years ago, when I was tasked with soliciting art to illustrate articles in *America* magazine. When I wondered aloud where I might find good Catholic art, a friend said, "Do you know about Brother Mickey?" and showed me a few prayer cards that he kept in his Bible. I was hooked. Mickey's art—whether the subject is Jesus, the Holy Family, the saints, or even general spiritual concepts like gratitude, freedom, or vocation—is a rare combination of beauty, inspiration, and joy. Especially joy. His images burst with color and energy, and make one feel happy not only to be a believer—but to be alive.

Brother Mickey is also a gifted speaker, much in demand across the country, where in parishes and schools and retreat houses and conferences he invites participants into the faith using color and line and shape. Mickey encourages everyone to come to know God, through the use of joyful images.

That's why this newest book is such a perfect fit. Has there ever been a more joyful evangelist than John XXIII? Although Pope Francis gives him a run for his money! Comfortable joking about appearance ("God knew from all eternity that I would be pope—why couldn't he have made me better looking?"), about his election as pope "(Anybody can be the pope: the proof is that I have become one.)", and about the Vatican bureaucracy (Journalist to Pope St. John XXIII: "How many people work in the Vatican?" John XXIII: "About half of them."), John was an accessible and inviting religious leader.

But John was not simply a roly-poly, jolly old man. Deeply learned in the faith and widely versed in international affairs, John helped to "open the windows" of the church with the modernizing and reforming Second Vatican Council. Much of what we are today in the church is thanks to his vision. In turn, Mickey's new book helps to "open the windows" of John's own saintly life through these arresting new images .

One more thing I'd like to say about Mickey: I'm grateful to him for introducing me to the spirituality of St. Francis de Sales, who is also quoted liberally in this delightful new volume. I'm embarrassed to say that I didn't know much about Francis's warm, humane and utterly sensible spirituality before knowing Mickey; but I am also delighted to say that, thanks to Mickey, he is one of my favorite saints.

Shortly after I told Mickey how much I was enjoying a book he had recommended on Francis, he sent me one of his lovely prayer cards with a Salesian quote on it: "Be who you are and be that perfectly well." This is of course the essence of sanctity: being the person God calls you to be, no more—but, more importantly, no less.

I pray that Mickey's new book will show you, through these new and beautiful images, how Saint John XXIII embodied that quote, and also how God calls us all to be the joyful evangelists of a new and beautiful world.

James Martin, SJ, is a Jesuit priest and author of many books, including *Jesus: A Pilgrimage.*

Life couldn't get any

better for American Catholics in the early sixties: Schools and churches were overflowing; Jack and Jackie Kennedy were in the White House with their two children (and since my mother's name was Jackie, the First Family was even more revered in our home); and Pope John XXIII (1881 – 1963) was opening wide his grandfatherly arms to embrace the entire world. Even a first grader such as I could not ignore the frenzy of universal affection and enthusiasm Pope St. John generated when he opened all those windows in the Vatican.

I also remember the shadow side of the euphoria—the ongoing Cold War and the Cuban Missile Crisis. Air raid drills and fallout shelters filled my six-year old imagination with panic during this brief but scary time. On October 11, 1962 in the midst of the international crisis, Pope John XXIII opened Vatican II, the most significant event of the Roman Catholic Church in modern times. Television brought war and peace into our living rooms on the evening news, each signaling the end of an old world order and the emergence of something new and daringly different. Half a century later, in a whole new millennium, we are still reeling from the effects of that time, struggling to make things work peacefully across even greater divides.

In 1974, eleven years after Pope John's death, and filled with Vatican II fervor, I joined the Oblates of St. Francis de Sales as a religious brother. Salesian spirituality, derived from the teachings and writings of St. Francis de Sales, is a way to God through peace of mind and loving friendships, highlighting the little virtues such as gentleness, cheerfulness, and patience. It is timeless, practical, and extremely challenging. Our unofficial community motto, written by de Sales himself is, "Be who you are and be that perfectly well." We Oblates embrace our full humanity, even the sinful parts.

I was overjoyed to learn as a young novice that de Sales was one of Pope John's favorite saints and Doctors of the Church, beginning in his seminary days when he first read *The Introduction to the Devout Life*, standard reading in all seminaries at that time. He loved St. Francis' practical, down-to-earth wisdom, his joyful optimism, and his keen understanding of the human heart. And since Francis was the first major spiritual writer to promote true devotion for laypeople, it is easy to see his influence on Pope John in calling Vatican II.

Fifty years after Pope John's death, Pope Francis has similarly captivated the world with his charm, humility, and his ecumenical devotion to all people, especially those living in the margins of poverty and alienation. His pronouncements against clericalism, his determination to clean house, his promotion of the dignity of women, gay people, and children, and his unflagging joyfulness in the midst of it all echo the spirits of these two great saints. How fitting that Pope Francis is responsible for John's canonization in April 2014, alongside Pope John Paul II, the pope who beatified John in 2000!

Hopefully, this collection of drawings, cartoons, and quotations will inspire the same optimism and "aggiornamento" (the spirit of moving forward) that characterized Pope St. John's prophetic life. That spirit filled the heart of St. Francis de Sales, who lived through the religious and social upheaval in the days following the Reformation. Time and again he called for dialogue and peaceful discourse, promoted love over fear, and encouraged prayerful devotion in the hearts of the faithful. That

same spirit is what prompted John to convene Vatican II, and is evident once again in the words and actions of Pope Francis, our first pope formed by Vatican II but not present at it. Each of these three men, in his own way, reminds us that nothing is more life-affirming, or more life-giving, than our humble acceptance of God's tender love and mercies.

But I must mention two other figures, both artists, whose works also offer a fascinating look at Pope St. John XXIII. Frederick Franck was a renowned American artist, a Quaker, who, out of devotion to Pope St. John and his prophetic message of peace, traveled to Rome uninvited to be present at the Vatican Council. In his book, *Outsider at the Vatican*, he says, "My response to Pope John's call had been to grab my sketchbook and to draw his council. I could not react as a theologian or liturgist, but only as one whose eyes were involved, an observer, and whose spirit and heart were open." His beautiful drawings and watercolors of the proceedings and the cardinals and bishops who sat for him also record the progression of Pope John's illness and last days— devastating for Franck to observe.

The other artist is Giacomo Manzu, the world-renowned Italian sculptor who created the bronze "Doors of Death" at the entrance of St. Peter's Basilica, and who became the official artist and sculptor of the Pope. In their private sessions together, the gentle pope and the communist atheist forged a deep and beautiful friendship in the face of bitter opposition from the curia. It was Manzu who was summoned in the middle of the night to create the clay death mask of his dear friend. Each of these artists reveals in his unique way the depth of beauty inside Pope St. John's heart and soul in ways that history books cannot.

In celebration of Pope St. John's canonization, I decided to illuminate some of my favorite quotes and anecdotes from him, highlighting those that also capture the spirit of the two Francises, whose quotes are also sprinkled throughout. So here they are on the same pages: Two popes and a saint OR two saints and a pope!

If you are serious about maintaining inner peace in the face of all your stress and anxiety, let me gently suggest a way for you to pray every morning: pour yourself a cup of coffee or tea, sit in a comfortable chair, acknowledge God's presence with a prayer of thanks, open this book to a page that makes you smile, and for just ten or fifteen minutes, pay attention to the dawn of a new Pentecost breaking open within you. Then, off you go, bringing the Holy Spirit and a small trail of peace, creativity, and joy into our weary world.

GOOD

SAINT

JOHN

XXIII

"We can ask St. Francis de Sales, the
Doctor of Sweetness, to give us the
grace to make bridges with others,
never walls." [1]
Pope Francis

"No one of the recent Doctors of
the Church more than St. Francis
de Sales anticipated the delibera-
tions and decisions of the Second
Vatican Council with such keen
and progressive insight." [2]

Pope Paul VI

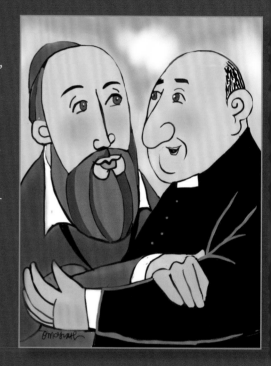

ST. FRANCIS de SALES

(1567-1622)

Patron of writers, journalists, and the Catholic press, St. Francis de Sales, the "Gentleman Saint," is one of the giants in the history of Christian spirituality. He was born and lived in Annecy, a town in the French Alps near the Swiss border, at the time of the Catholic Reformation. Francis's classic work is the *Introduction to the Devout Life*, which remains a bestseller to this day. In it, he suggests a practical, down-to-earth way for all people, especially the laity, to discover their own spiritual path.

Cheerfulness, optimism, and a refusal to be dominated by stress and anxiety through the practice of the little virtues are hallmarks of Salesian spirituality, and the very ones which Pope St. John found so attractive. Francis de Sales was a man of even-tempered peace who sought open, respectful dialogue with all people, even his Calvinist foes in Geneva, where he was the Catholic bishop but was forbidden to enter the city. These aspects of his life are what so strongly influenced Pope St. John's passion for ecumenism, reconciliation, and peace.

ANGELO RONCALLI

LATER POPE JOHN XXIII

Angelo Roncalli was born on November 25, 1881, in a small town in northern Italy called Sotto Il Monte. One of ten children, he was the son of very poor farmers who were richly blessed with love and faith. At the age of fourteen, as a seminarian, Angelo began the life-long practice of keeping a prayer journal, which was published after his death under the title *Journal of a Soul*.

Following a year of military service, Angelo was ordained a priest in 1904, and served as secretary to a bishop devoted to social justice and workers' rights. Bishop Tedeschi became Angelo's great mentor and life-long inspiration. After serving as an army chaplain in World War I and witnessing firsthand the horrors of war, Angelo rose in the church ranks and perfected his natural gift for diplomacy.

In 1925, he was consecrated a bishop and sent as a papal envoy to Bulgaria, where for the next ten years he worked tirelessly at mending relations with the Orthodox church. It was a desperately lonely position in a rugged country where he felt little support from anyone. But he carried on with joy and optimism nonetheless. By the time of his departure ten years later, he had won over many hearts and learned how to move forward in the face of strong opposition.

Bishop Roncalli next served the church as an apostolic delegate to Greece and Turkey in 1935, a position he held until the end of World War II. Once again, his great diplomatic skills and his profound love for the gospels helped him to break down barriers with Orthodox Christians, Turkish Muslims, and Jews, thousands of whom he helped escape Nazi persecution.

In 1944, Pope Pius XII appointed Angelo Roncalli the Papal Nuncio to France, a very important position in those postwar days of rebuilding a nation and reconciling with former enemies. Before long he was widely known and loved in Paris and beyond.

In 1953, Bishop Roncalli was appointed the cardinal patriarch of Venice. He loved Venice, and the Venetians adored him. He once remarked that Venice gave him a foretaste of heaven, which made it that much sadder to leave there in 1958 when he was elected pope and transformed the church. No one was more surprised than he.

"A church without prophets falls into the trap of clericalism. When clericalism reigns supreme, true believers weep because they cannot find the Lord." [3]

Pope Francis

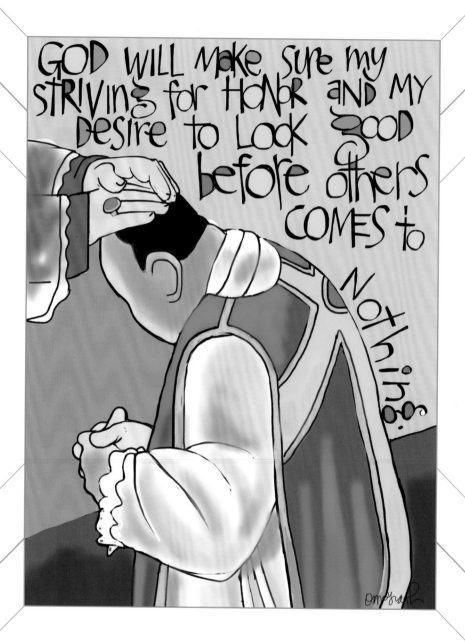

GOOD

SAINT

JOHN

XXIII

Angelo Roncalli entered the seminary in
Bergamo, Italy in 1892. He finished his
seminary education and doctoral studies in
Rome, where he was ordained a priest on
August 10, 1904.

"Bishops must be pastors, close to their people, not men who behave like little princes." [4]

Pope Francis

I'm like a bird singing in a thicket of thorns.

deSales

Pope John loved this quote from de Sales as a way to explain how he handled stress.

"I spent the day in the company of SFS, my gentlest of saints. If I were like him, I would not even mind if they made me Pope. By the light of his example, I feel more inclined toward humility, gentleness, and inner calm." [5] (1902)

"Oh my loving saint, there is so much I would say to you. I love you tenderly and will always look to you for help. You can see into my heart, give me what I need to become like you." [6] (1902)

"I will always remember St. Francis' advice: Do not get anxious when the waves batter against your boat. Have no fear while God is with you." [7] (Easter retreat, 1903)

"I must desire not to be what I am not, but to be very truly what I really am. That is what my St. Francis de Sales tells me." [8] (1909)

"Oh, if I could only be like St. Francis de Sales in everything! To be meek and humble of heart is still the brightest glory of a bishop and papal representative." [9] (1947)

All of these quotes are from Pope St. John's entries in *Journal of a Soul*, which he began writing in 1896.

"Choose saints in whose intercession you have confidence." [10]

– St. Francis de Sales

After eleven ballots,

Angelo Roncalli was elected pope on October 28, 1958. Many of the cardinals who voted for him did so thinking that he would be a quiet caretaker Pope. From the moment he announced that his name would be JOHN, after 200 years of popes named Pius and Benedict, it was clear that this was a man who would not be afraid to fly in the face of tradition.

He chose the name John because it was the name of two men very close to Jesus: John the Baptist, who announced Christ's birth and was later martyred; and John the Evangelist, whose gospel emphasizes love and unity most profoundly in Jesus's final discourse.

"I will be called John. The name is dear to me because it was the name of my father and the humble parish church where we were baptized." [11]

"I shall be called John, a sweet, gentle, solemn name." [12]

"There have been 22 pontiffs named John, nearly all have had a brief pontificate." [13]

"I am not a good-looking pope—just look at my ears—but you will get along well with me." [14]

"Being pope today can turn your hair as white as your soutaine." [15]
(on the election of Pius XII)

"We must shake off the imperial dust that has gathered on the throne of Peter since Constantine." [16]

"Tradition means protect the fire, not preserve the ashes." [17]

Pope St. John is

the first pope of the television age, and the media loved this rotund, gentle grandfather of a pope who loved to be out and about, visiting prisons, children's hospitals, and now, through the wonders of modern technology, living rooms around the world.

Pope Francis finds himself in an even more advanced and accelerated period of progress, which he speaks of often. Like John, he is a darling of the media.

GOOD

SAINT

JOHN

XXIII

"Ever since I saw myself made pope, thanks to TV, I attach a great importance to it." [18]   *Pope St. John XXIII*

"The Catholic world is moving very fast. The important thing is to open a dialogue so that Rome can catch up with everyone else." [19]   *Pope St. John XXIII*

"The most important possibility for the use of digital communications is the proclamation of the Gospel." [20]
Pope Francis

"I am the pastor of a church without frontiers." [21]
Pope Francis

"Let our communication be a balm which relieves pain and a fine wine that gladdens hearts. Let us boldly become citizens of the digital world." [22]
Pope Francis

"The internet must be used to meet real people, who are often hurting or lost, and offer real reasons for hope." [23]
Pope Francis

GOOD

SAINT

JOHN

XXIII

· ·

"I am the gardener of the world,
but rather than weeding, I am
watering what is growing." [24]

Pope St. John XXIII

· ·

XXIII

Pope St. John's

earthiness was rooted in the fact that he was born into a poor family of peasant farmers—and it was always a source of great pride for him. This deep connection to na-ture and its ongoing cycles of life and death was at the very heart of everything he said, wrote, and did. For him, the Ecumenical Council was the sign of a new and univer-sal spring, the dawn of a new age in the world and a new Pentecost in the church.

"The church is a multi-colored garden." [26]
St. Francis de Sales

"We are not meant to be museum keepers, but to cultivate a flourishing garden of life." [27]
Pope St. John XXIII

"I have never known a pessimist to accomplish anything useful." [28]
Pope St. John XXIII

"I would like to open the Vatican gardens to children so they would have somewhere to hide, to dig tunnels, to play in the woods instead of the dangerous streets. But it would mean changing some rules, and that requires someone stronger than the pope." [29]

Pope St. John XXIII

. . . .

"Nothing should have the power
to take away our peace." [30]

St. Francis de Sales

. . . .

Pope John desperately missed the freedom
to walk the streets of Rome and actually meet
real people with real problems and concerns.
Unfortunately, he had to settle for taking his
daily walks in the Vatican gardens. However,
unlike his predecessors, he didn't insist that
the workers evacuate the premises when he
strolled—he loved to engage them in con-
versation, ask about their families, and even
gave all Vatican employees a raise after ask-
ing the gardener one day how much he was
being paid.

When he was Archbishop Bergoglio, Pope Francis loved to ride buses and subways to meet and mingle with regular people.

41

"Here in the Vatican they don't like their bishop to walk anywhere except in the back garden, where they can keep an eye on me like a prisoner." [31]
Pope St. John XXIII

"For my health's sake… it will do me good to go out for a walk everyday. O Lord, I find this hard and it seems such a waste of time, but still it is necessary, and everybody insists that I should do so, so I shall do it, offering the Lord the effort it costs me." [32]
Pope St. John XXIII

"The spirit of truth, of peace, always hovers over this world and stretches its wings over our heads in order to wake in us the same wonder which at the beginning of time made the entire universe palpitate with new life." [33]
Pope St. John XXIII

"I feel like an empty sack which the Holy Spirit suddenly and forcefully fills." [34]
Pope St. John XXIII

Pope St. John's days

usually began with prayer at four in the morning. He could never have accomplished all that he did, with such joy and enthusiasm, were he not a man of prayer and contemplation. He had a truly mystic spirit which recognized God and God alone as the source and summit of our inner peace and serenity. For John, prayer and peace (both personal inner peace as well as world peace), went hand in hand.

The motto he chose to define his life as priest, bishop, and pope was "OBEDIENCE AND PEACE." Discovering the will of God in his life—and more importantly, obeying it—was of utmost importance. That is how he maintained the inner peace he needed to navigate the church through such rocky times.

"My soul is comforted with confidence in the New Pentecost." [36]
Pope St. John XXIII

"Obedience and peace. There lies the secret to my successes." [37]
Pope St. John XXIII

"God is doing something in me even though I do not see it or feel it." [38]
Pope St. John XXIII

"Patience and calm, two beautiful qualities." [39]
Pope St. John XXIII

"Prayer is a matter of drawing God's heart and eyes to us." [35]

Pope Francis

· ·

GOOD

SAINT

JOHN

XXIII

. . . .

"Prayer goes so well at first light,
when everything is quiet." [40]

Pope St. John XXIII

. . . .

"Morning prayer opens the window of
your spirit to the Sun of Justice." [41]
St. Francis de Sales

"The more you pray, the more you
want to pray." [42]
Pope St. John XXIII

"Every morning, before anything else,
ask God for gentleness of spirit." [43]
St. Francis de Sales

"I must give time to meditation and
stay longer in the Lord's company." [44]
Pope St. John XXIII

"Pure prayer is listening to God, conversing with God, and being silent before God." [45]

Pope St. John XXIII

"We have to listen to the Spirit. It's within each one of us. What does the Holy Spirit tell us? That God is good, that God loves us, that God always forgives." [46]

Pope Francis

GOOD

SAINT

JOHN

XXIII

"Let some fresh air into
the church." [47]

Pope St. John XXIII

Acting on what he felt

was a burst of inspiration from the Holy Spirit in 1959, Pope John called an Ecumenical Council, commonly called Vatican II, to bring the church into the modern world, to open the windows and let in the fresh air of sweeping reform. This most momentous event in modern church history finally opened on October 11, 1962.

John said that the purpose of the council was "aggiornamento," an Italian word which suggests bringing up to date. And once again drawing on his gardening metaphor, he said that the inspiration for this "New Pentecost" sprang up like a flower in an unexpected springtime.

XXIII

"I was the first to be astonished about my own proposal, nobody had ever given me such ideas. The idea of an Ecumenical Council was not the ripe fruit of long consider-ations, it just occurred to us as the surprising blossom of an unexpect-ed spring...the result of a sponta-neous inspiration." [48]

Pope St. John XXIII

"Without some holy madness, the church cannot grow." [49]

Pope St. John XXIII

"Perhaps the church appears too dis-tant from people's needs, too cold. Perhaps too caught up with itself, a prisoner of its own rigid formulas. Perhaps the world has made the church a relic of the past, unfit for new questions." [50]

Pope Francis

"We must go where inspiration impels us."

"Follow only those inspirations that are holy and bring you peace." [51]

St. Francis de Sales

"The council now beginning rises in the church like daybreak, a forerunner of most splendid light." [52]
Pope St. John XXIII

"We must declare our total disagreement with those prophets of doom who always foretell catastrophes as though the world were close to its end." [53]
Pope St. John XXIII in his opening address.

GOOD

SAINT

JOHN

XXIII

. . . .

"I try to pull out a brick here and there" [54]

Pope St. John XXIII in Bulgaria

. . . .

Pope St. John was a

natural-born diplomat whose main concern was creating unity in the midst of diversity. He believed that simply talking to each other, not debating, and building friendly relationships were the very foundations of world peace. One of the intentions of the Ecumenical Council was to heal the Church's long-broken relations with Orthodox Christians and Protestants.

"May Christ enflame the desires of all men to break through the barriers which divide them, to strengthen the bonds of mutual love, to learn to understand one another, and to pardon those who have done them wrong." [55]
Pope John, in Pacem in Terris

XXIII

"To change the world we must change ourselves." [56]
St. Francis de Sales

"I have always been more concerned with what unites than with what separates." [57]
Pope St. John XXIII

"The future is in the respectful co-existence of diversity." [58]

Pope Francis

INRI

GOOD

SAINT

JOHN

XXIII

"This is the mystical Body
of Christ." [60]

Pope St. John XXIII

upon seeing newsreel footage of
Bergen Belsen Concentration Camp

One of the most

groundbreaking documents to emerge from Vatican II was "Nostra Aetate" (In Our Time), which, for the first time in two thousand years of Christianity, addressed people of faiths and cultures other than Christian and removed from Jews the blame for Christ's death.

During World War II, as papal nuncio in Istanbul, John was responsible for rescuing thousands of Jewish lives through visas acquired with the help of various diplomats, the Sisters of Sion, and King Boris of Bulgaria and fake baptismal certificates.

Like Pope John Paul II, John had a deep and abiding love for the Jewish people and was determined to heal the rifts between Jews and Christians. As pope, he formed a commission to study the history of their relations and had 120 private audiences with Jewish groups and representatives.

"Poor children of Israel. Daily I hear their groans around me. They are relatives and fellow countrymen of Jesus. May the divine savior come to their aid." [61]
Pope St. John XXIII

"I am your brother, Joseph." [62]
Pope John to American Jewish leaders who presented him with a Torah

"Forgive us, Lord, for the curse we falsely attributed to their name as Jews. Forgive us for crucifying Thee a second time in their flesh. For we know not what we did." [63]
Pope St. John XXIII

"Are we still a church capable of leading people back to Jerusalem? Jerusalem is where our roots are." [64]
Pope Francis

Considered the greatest

papal encyclical of modern times, Pacem in Terris was written at the height of the Cold War between communism and the free world. In it, Pope John XXIII not only addressed the ever-looming threat of nuclear war and the need for all nations to be free and self-determining, but he addressed worker's rights, civil rights, women's rights, and the immorality of racial discrimination and exploitation.

As he was writing it, Pope John was haunted by a memory from his days as a chaplain in the Italian Army during World War I: an Austrian soldier screaming in anguish after being shot in the chest. This painful image stayed with John all his life and fed his determination to promote world peace.

XXIII

"Every believer must be a spark of light, a nucleus of love, a leaven for the whole mass." [65]

"There can be no peace between men until there is peace within each one of them." [66]

"The world will never be the dwelling place of peace until peace has found a home in each and every heart." [67]

"Let us bet on hope, and the hope for peace, and it will be possible." [68]

Pope Francis

. . . .

"Old age must be a source of tranquil inner joy." [69]

Pope St. John XXIII

. . . .

SIMPLIFY
everything.

Pope St. John loved to point out that he was born poor, and that he would die poor. While his entire life was characterized by his love for simplicity and a spirit of detachment, these humble qualities reached their perfection in his last years after he had spent a lifetime mastering them.

XXIII

"I keep feeling my heart to see if advancing age is making me mean. Age frees me from care and detaches my heart." [70]
St. Francis de Sales

"As for little troubles, take them as they come, keep calm and peaceful, and thank the Lord they are not worse." [72]
Pope St. John XXIII

"The older I get, the more I realize the value of simplicity in thought, word, and speech…simplify all that is complex." [73]
Pope St. John XXIII

"The older I grow, surrounded by worldly greatness and honor, the more I am drawn to the greatest simplicity." [74]
Pope St. John XXIII

· ·

"Mt. Calvary is the school
of love." [75]

St. Francis de Sales

· ·

Underlying the genuine

joy and warm affection on the surface of Pope St. John's life was a profound love for the crucifix which he carried in his heart. He would not have been able to accomplish all that he did, with such hope, were it not for his loving embrace of the suffering Christ.

"Do you know why I keep that crucifix opposite my bed? It is there so that I can see it first thing in the morn- ing, and the last thing at night. It is there so that I can talk to it during the long evening hours. Those open arms have been the program of my pontificate, a modest and humble one. Those open arms say to me that they are the church because Christ died for all, no one excepted." [76]
Pope St. John XXIII

"In my nightly conversations with the Lord, I always have before me Jesus crucified, His arms outstretched to receive everyone." [77]
Pope St. John XXIII

"The secret to my ministry is that cru- cifix you see opposite my bed. Those open arms say that Christ dies for all. No one is excluded from His love and forgiveness." [78]
Pope St. John XXIII

· ·

"Learn to embrace your crosses." [79]

St. Francis de Sales

· ·

"I want to be wholly for God, penetrated with His light, shining with love for God and souls." [80]
Pope St. John XXIII

"If you only knew how I suffer because so many men believe that the church condemns them. I do as He does. I open my arms and love." [81]
Pope St. John to the Archbishop of Cambrai

Just one month before

the Council opened in October of 1962, Pope St. John was diagnosed with incurable stomach cancer. While the disease got progressively worse, forcing him to cancel private audiences and appointments, it did not stop him from watching the sessions of the council on closed-circuit television, nor from writing "Pacem in Terris". He died on June 3, 1963, the day after Pentecost.

This drawing is a copy of one by Frederick Franck. Sketched during the pope's last public appearence in St. Peter's, he was deeply distressed to see the condition of the once vibrant pope whom he so loved and admired.

"I am aware of certain disturbances in my body that must be natural for an old man. I bear with it calmly, even if it does give me a little annoyance at times." [82]
Pope St. John XXIII

"Pain is no foe of mine. Wonderful memories give me great joy now and fill my life. There is really no room for pain." [83]
Pope St. John XXIII

"Now I understand what contributions to the Council the Lord requires of me: suffering." [84]
Pope St. John XXIII

"I await the arrival of Sister Death calmly and gladly. I shall welcome her." [85]
Pope St. John XXIII

"This bed is an altar. An altar calls for a victim. Here I am, ready. I am at peace." [86]
Pope St. John XXIII

"The bed of the sick is an altar of sacrifice." [87]

St. Francis de Sales

"I have launched this great ship. Others will have to bring it into port." [88]

Pope St. John XXIII

Pope John died of stomach cancer on June 3, 1963. Intense pain did not dampen his resolve to die in the light of Christ's love. His last clear words were, "Lord, you know that I love you." His cherished family and friends, including his devoted personal assistant, Monsignor Loris Capovilla, surrounded his bed while outside thousands of people gathered to pray for him at Mass in St. Peter's Square. John died at the very same moment as the final blessing: "The Mass is ended. Go in peace."

Pope John was beatified in 2000 by Pope John Paul II. In his homily that day, Pope John Paul said, "Everyone remembers the image of Pope John's smiling face and two outstretched arms embracing the whole world."

In 2014, Pope Francis honored Loris Capovilla, then in his 90's, by naming him a Cardinal.

Pope Francis canonized Good Pope John along with Pope John Paul II on April 27, 2014.

THE **LIGHTER SIDE** OF

SOURCES AND ACKNOWLEDGMENTS

SOURCES FOR QUOTES FROM POPE JOHN XXIII

Journal of a Soul
Pope John XXIII
Geoffrey Chapman, London, 1964
5, 6, 7, 8, 9

The Heart and Mind of John XXIII:
His Secretary's Intimate Recollection
Loris Capovilla
Hawthorn Books, 1964
12, 57

"Pacem in Terris"
54, 65, 66, 67

Pope John XXIII: Essential Writings
Ed. By Jean Maalouf
Orbis Press, 2008
40, 81

Lives of the Popes
Richard P. McBrien
Harper San Francisco, 1997
13, 27, 52, 88

Outsider in the Vatican
Frederick Franck
Macmillan, 1965
16, 24, 33

JFK and the Unspeakable
James Douglass
Orbis Press, 2008
83

An Artist and the Pope
Curtis Bill Pepper
Peter Davies, London 1968
29, 31, 48, 76, 82, 86

A Joyful Soul: Messages From a
Saint for Our Times
Ed. By Jerome Vereb, CP
Andrews McMeel Publishers, 2000
32, 36, 38, 42, 44, 69, 71, 72, 73, 74, 78, 80

My Heart Speaks:
Wisdom from Pope John
Ed. Jeanne Kuhn
The Word Among Us
37, 84

The Good Pope: John XXIII and
Vatican II
Greg Tobin
Harper One, 2012
11, 15

Overlook Much, Correct Little
Ed. By Rothlin Hans-Peter
New City Press, 2007
14, 17, 28, 34, 49

A Pope John Memorial Miniature:
Wit, Faith , Prayer, Eulogies
Random House
18, 37, 39, 77

SOURCES FOR QUOTES FROM ST. FRANCIS DE SALES

Introduction to the Devout Life
St. Francis de Sales
Ed. By John K. Ryan
Doubleday, 1972
10

Treatise on the Love of God
St. Francis de Sales
Ed. By John K. Ryan
Tan Publishers, 1974
26

A Testimony by St. Chantal
Elizabeth Stoppe
Institute of Salesian Studies, 1967
63,70

Finding God's Will for You
St. Francis de Sales
Sophia Institute Press, 1991
25, 51, 79

Salesian Spirituality: A Sourcebook for Inspiration
Noel Rebello, MSFS
SFS Publications, 2004
41, 43

SOURCES FOR QUOTES FROM POPE FRANCIS

Evangelii Gaudium
Pope Francis
21

Homily, January 24, 2014 (World Communications Day/ Memorial of SFS)
1, 22, 23

Homilies
3 (12-17-13), 35, 50 (to Brazilian Bishops), 58 (Nov 28, 2013 at the Plenary Assembly for the Pontifical Council for Inter-religious Dialogue), 68 (First Sunday Advent, 2013)

Rome Reports
46

Quote #2 from Pope Paul VI is from a 1967 apostolic letter commemorating the four hundredth anniversary of the birth of St. Francis de Sales.

I found each of the following books exceptionally helpful in my understanding of Pope John's life and legacy.

The Good Pope
Greg Tobin
Harper One, 2012

I Will Be Called John
Lawrence Elliott
Berkley Medallion Books, 1973

Pope John XXIII
Peter Hebblethwaite
Doubleday, 1985

Watching the Vatican: Perceptions of Frederick Franck
Valkhof Press, 1999

Practicing Catholic
James Carroll
Houghton Mifflin Harcourt, 2009

What happened at Vatican II
John W. O'Malley
Belknap/ Harvard University Press 2008

My Heart Speaks: Wisdom From Pope
John XXIII
The Word Among Us Press, 2000

I once had the great

honor of sharing a meal with the late Archbishop Dennis Hurley of South Africa, a giant of the modern Catholic church. A gregarious, warm-hearted Irishman, he readily answered questions and shared memories of his entire fascinating career as a bishop with those of us gathered. I, of course, wanted to hear all about his experience of attending Vatican II and actually meeting Pope John face to face. He told us that when he was first presented to him, Pope John opened his arms wide open and simply said, "Tell me something good. Everyone else fills me with bad news, so I want to hear something happy from you."

Thus, my words of thanks go to Archbishop Hurley, who through his firsthand reports, fanned the flames of my deep regard for Pope John XXIII. I wish he had lived to see him canonized, but I am sure he'll be watching the proceedings from a better vantage point.

I loved growing spiritually closer to Good Pope John throughout the course of working on this project—and could never have done it alone. I would like to express sincere and loving thanks to **Jim Knipper**, my friend and publisher, who masterfully oversees the details for me; to **Doug Cordes**, the wonderful designer who turned my raw materials into this gem of a book; to **Jim Martin, SJ** for the sincere heaps of enthusiastic praise in his foreword; and to my **Oblate confreres**, especially my provincial, **Jim Greenfield**, **OSFS** with whom I share deep love for all things de Sales.

Bro. Michael O'Neill McGrath, OSFS lives and works in Camden, NJ. In addition to publishing books which feature his artwork and texts, Bro. Mickey gives retreats and presentations to a wide array of groups around the country. In keeping with Pope St. John's personal practice of morning prayer, he frequently shares devotional illustrations for meditation on his facebook page, bromickeymcgrath. Books, prints, and cards are available on his website, www.bromickeymcgrath.com.